Tarot & Oracle

365 Day Challenge

For Busy Souls

By Ouassima Touahria

Powered by

Casa Magik

Title: Tarot & Oracle 365 Day Challenge, For Busy Souls.

ISBN : 9798676510817

Ouassima Touahria

Powered by CoreMagik ©2020 Copyright reserved in all countries

coremagik@gmail.com

Creation: Ouassima Touahria

Book Cover Art: Evgenia Veselkova from "Nest of Light Oracle"

Design: Ouassima Touahria

Icon's creation: Iris

Linguistic revision: Silvia "MoonCoach" Pancaro, Cilla Conway, Elisabeth.B

The content of this book is intended for people who wish to make personal and spiritual development, change their lives and continue their path of ascension in the best possible way for them. The content of this book is not a substitute for any care or treatment offered by health professionals but is the personal opinion of the author.

For busy souls who wish to reconnect with their divinity

...

May this journey be profound and transformative for you...

"These challenges made me think in different ways about the Tarot and opened up my intuition for using them. They inspired me to see the decks as friends rather than just tools.

I would suggest them to potential tarot readers because they are easy for beginners to follow and then they lead them gently into new card territories." Luci D. Davies

"Being invited to spend a considerable amount of time with just one deck (or one theme), and to approach it from different vantage points, offers the potential for developing a deep appreciation for that deck. You may even end up feeling the kind of love that The Little Prince felt for his rose! I was surprised at how deeply I bonded with a deck that I had almost decided to part with!

These challenges also allow you to "test" your deck for questions you would never have considered asking, or that no querent would even ask! How often have I sat there scratching my head and thinking "there is no way the cards could possibly answer this question", but time and time again they delivered an answer!

By following a line of questioning that may be different from what comes naturally to you, you are opening your heart and your mind, and you will see your world expand in unexpected ways." M. Nelson

Before we start

Why this book?

Hi dear souls and welcome to this journey!

As card lovers, we are passionate about Tarot or Oracles. We are curious about them and have this strong attraction and desire to know our decks better and discover their mysteries... However, life can get pretty busy and we get lost between our obligations and aspirations. We push our passions away hoping to have time in the future... "Maybe one day, when I have some time, I will play with this deck, I will study this subject, I will sit with myself..." But that "Rendez-vous" doesn't come as more and more tasks are added to the "Must Do" list ...

Create this time!

So, I created this book to give you the opportunity:

- To practice reading even if you don't have much time: This book is indeed ... for busy souls!
- To know your decks better
- To know yourself better
- To get in touch with yourself in a personal and dedicated space
- To explore important subjects, and reflect on fun and serious topics
- To restructure your life, and bring more balance and harmony
- To embrace your truths
- And to read for others if you want to!

This book offers practical and fun exercises, short and sweet that you can do within whatever time you have in your day. Whether you have 5 minutes or want to take an hour a day to dive deeper into your study, it's up to you. The principles are simple: having a spiritual practice while having fun and evolving. Even if you don't have much time, you can still learn and use your decks!

What if you do not have time? My goal is to help you practice daily for 5 minutes or more; that's why there are no obligations or strict rules. If you do the challenges in the given periods, that's perfect. If you have more or less time, that's ok too! If you don't follow the pace, don't blame yourself; instead, use this energy to do more exercises and join Facebook groups to do these exercises with other students and card lovers.

Questions?

Before we start, I want to give you some notes to help you benefit from this book in the best way:

- Always have your cards with you, while exploring the challenges, and pick cards whenever you see a question mark!

- I suggest you use what you already have – whether Tarot or Oracle decks – these challenges work with both systems.

- How to start? Even if I have created this book in a certain order, you do not have to follow it day by day or month by month, follow your own pace and time.

- *Do I need to know how Tarot or Oracle systems work?* It may help and this book is an opportunity to learn to read Tarot or Oracles in a non-conventional way. There is no problem! Questions and spreads can speak to any level card reader. We encourage you to jump in because we have to start somewhere, right?

- *Do I need to have a specific deck to do the exercises?* In case you do the challenges alone: NO. If you do it in a group, it is better that you focus on one deck at a time to get to know it in depth. You can find these groups on Facebook like our Facebook group: *"Study your tarot deck in 21 days."* I suggest you don't jump onto Amazon or Etsy to get any new decks; use those that you already have and explore them as every deck is full of treasures.

- *Can I use different Oracles and Tarot decks at the same time?* That's your choice and that's totally fine! You can use Oracles and Tarot decks as combos! You may want to use the same deck for a week before jumping to another, or the same deck every Friday, etc. There are many creative ways to use the decks so try to find your own way.

● *The deck I have doesn't speak to me!* Don't panic! It can happen, so ask yourself: Is this deck for me? Am I having an Oracle/Tarot burnout? Do the images speak to me? Or do I want different exercises for this week? In all cases, give the deck some time; you might get back to it within weeks, months, or years - this happens to me, too! If after all, it doesn't speak to you, I suggest you get to know yourself better and ask yourself: What do I like? What images move me? What is my goal at the moment? What images/colors enhance my psychic abilities?

● You can always trade your decks in the trade groups online to get a better tarot for you.

I sincerely hope this book helps you in many ways and that it adds more passion and harmony to your life.

Ouassima Issare

What is Divination

Divination is associated with magic, witchcraft, shamanism and many other practices and traditions.

Divination is for me, a set of methods that we use to obtain divine guidance, a message, information, and wisdom by means that are considered supernatural.

Divination tools can be different from one tradition to another and from one person to another. Some forms of divination do not require tools, but depend on the person's natural psychic abilities and readiness to listen to messages. But it is possible to use certain objects to accentuate one's agility, or to open the doors of perception. The objects do not need to be sacred because we can use ordinary items such as bones or shells, etc.

Throughout history, Tarot and Oracles and their different forms, are considered tools of divination across many diverse Cultures.

Why Cards?

Card lovers use them for multiple reasons, to find answers, get to know each other better, explore serious and less serious subjects, and share life lessons like what we are about to do in this book. And there are many other reasons!

Among other things, the cards allow you to:

- Develop your creativity and talents, and find inspiration around an artistic activity
- Brainstorm for a project
- Initiate the path of writing
- Dive into a card and meditate with it, enter into its universe...
- Have the impression of visiting a museum or an art exhibition ...
- Enter another fantastic, magical universe, and return to ancient times...in short, there is something for everyone!

- Find your tribe, exchange with a community that shares the same passion

- See that a card understands you, that it reflects your emotional and mental state with its images ...

- Cards are a door to other areas of knowledge and pleasure: Astrology, Kabbalah, humor and more!

- Develop curiosity and patience

- Being with the cards simply gives you joy

- Receive and give cards as gifts, which strengthens ties and relationships and allows you to discover decks that you may not necessarily have bought!

- The fact of buying a deck for yourself, whether as a reward after a project or simply for the pleasure of giving yourself a gift, and the pleasure of planning the time allocated to discover the works of art that amaze you, having time with yourself, etc.

Meet with Oracles

An Oracle was a priest or priestess who practiced divination in ancient Greece, was in contact with gods and Goddesses, and provided prophecies and guidance. This word comes from the Latin word ōrāre, "to speak".

In the Bible, Oracle is the sanctuary of the Temple.

An interesting fact about this word: it is used in computer science: it is a black box that can give the correct answers.

What we call "Oracle cards" in our everyday world today are all the other card decks which provide and reveal messages, but which do not have the structure of the Tarot.

Oracle cards have several cards and a structure chosen by the creator's intention and inspiration.

You certainly know that the cards can help you develop your intuition, help you meditate, and so on. However, do you know they can help you develop your talents and creative gifts?

Oracles are in my opinion more creative, and fluid, *and offer* more variety. Each oracle card deck has its own universe which offers you multiple experiences and teaches you a lot about subjects you may not know.

We might think that the Tarot is a separate system from Oracle, but in my reality, the Oracle system is the Mother, and Tarot is the son. Tarot is an Oracle.

Let's begin

Fight Stereotypes in 11 Days

Despite the spiritual globalization and internet openness that makes us connected, and make knowledge available to us, I still see many people who approach cards like a sin! In secret, as we did with psychologists a few years ago.

In the next few days, we will explore stereotypes around cards, allowing you to free yourself from them. I want to encourage you to have a free and fun practice, so try this challenge to reflect on judgments you might have regarding cards in general and take this opportunity to adjust your inner position towards cards.

Day 1

Approaching cards depends on the religious and cultural background of the person; for example, in certain religions, one should not "see the future" because it is synonymous with "no faith in God." However, several prophets saw the future: one example is Joseph who had premonitory dreams, and another is Mohamed in Islam who gave predictions.

- How does my religious and cultural background impact my approach to cards?

- How do they influence my readings?

Day 2

In some cultures, drawing cards can be associated with witchcraft; those who draw the cards can practice magic and witchcraft, but they are different practices. Some card readers are not at all related to the field of witchcraft. It's like saying that all those who meditate are wizards!

- What is the link between cards and witchcraft?
- How do you want to be identified by people?
- What practices do you want to hide from others? Why?

Day 3

Drawing cards is synonymous with "reading fortunes". In the past, this association may have given chance to scammers who took advantage of people in need of solutions for desperate situations. this led people to be cautious and suspicious of card readers.

This has an impact on the reader's approach to clients: Some readers may want to impress others to build trust and attract clients; others might hide some important information because they are afraid of the client's reaction and judgment.

- What is the impact of this suspicion on your practice?
- What can you do about it?

Day 4

It's a hobby: reading can be fun, and we joke over it, but it can be very serious. I remember the time when we were with colleagues and we were having fun with the cards... and oops, a card jumped out and what I said about it made her face change completely. Some people will be afraid because the cards tell a Truth that they are not ready to hear. So, it becomes a dangerous mirror to avoid at all costs!

Hence the importance of having fun; we need to have the courage to see the truth and take action.

- If you were in a similar situation, how would you react?
- Will you be ready to use cards at parties?

Day 5

When a person decides to have a reading, it may be because she needs:

- To listen (active listening) to what is deeply hidden within her heart; she wants to put words to her feelings and thoughts, and she wants to connect to her deep desire.

- Clarity: when the situation is complicated and she is in darkness, she wants to see things with lucidity.

- Guidance: To know where she is going, what she should do next...

- To be reassured, to have more confidence ...

What are your needs when you look for a reading?

Day 6

Now, a serious question!

- Is Tarot linked to dark magic or white magic? Does it open the doors of hell?

- Is the Tarot supernatural?

- Is the Tibetan bowl supernatural? Are the crystals supernatural?

- What does it mean supernatural?

Day 7 If you feel ready!

Explore these questions and build your answers. We suggest addressing these questions with honesty if you feel courageous, to do so now. If not, you might come back to these questions when you have finished the other challenges after you've built your confidence:

- What is Hell? Am I afraid of darkness?

- What is Light? What represents light for me?

- What is the impact of this vision on my practice as a Tarot reader?

Day 8

I consider Card readers to be ordinary people, but with great sensitivity, they want to help people and came into the world with gifts to share. If you have a gift for cooking, you will not refuse it, hide it and tell yourself that it is a sin; on the contrary, you will use this gift to feed others and help them to live and taste life with their senses!

- What are my gifts as a Tarot/Oracle reader?

- How can I share them with others?

- If I put this in a brand, what would be its name, colors, and personality?

Day 9

We are not an open channel 24 hours long.

Each reader has his own pace, some can read in 10 minutes, others in one hour, etc. Some can read all day; others can't read beyond 2 or 3 people a day...

Everyone has their own way of reading, their own price like every other service and business, they each have a talent, an energy to transmit.

- What is your own pace of doing readings for yourself? Once a day? Once a week?

- What would be your pace if you do readings for others?

Day 10

I have identified 2 ways to approach cards among people (clients and sometimes readers) so far:

Old vision: There is one destiny - the person has no power, fears the future, lives in uncertainty, and has a logic of magic pills: give me the answer, but tell me not to change.

New vision: The person has a co-creative power - is honest with herself, and responsible. She respects free will so she does not ask questions like: what does he think of me?!

With this vision, we understand that we make a choice every second of our life, that there are cosmic influences, we talk about planets, astrology, other dimensions... We understand that everything is a mirror, whether signs and synchronicities, or decks and cards, everything is alive. The timelines change every second according to our actions and our intentions...

I am more aligned with the second vision and you might think that I constructed here my stereotype, but it helps me to identify my approach and communicate it to others. This shows my practice and my way of doing readings:

I seek inner harmony, and this is what brings me to take the right decisions.

- I look for external and internal factors and influencers...
- I believe in Light and Shadow but as part of Oneness.

What about you:

- What are your belief systems about destiny?
- About free will?
- Choice?

Day 11

We have learned to put intermediaries between us and everything around us!

For our bodies, we have the doctors who take care of them; for our money, the banks take care of it; for couples, it was the stepmothers, now it's TV and popular culture of "couple."

We have removed the figure of "Hierophant" but we kept his negative side, its logic is still here.

So don't let anyone tell you there is ONE way to read cards or you MUST start with the Rider Waite or the Marseille! Love yourself, love your vision, and trust your inner compass!

- What is the system that attracts you now?
- What do you fear about it? What is preventing you from approaching it?
- Regarding your practice: What would be the 1st step to take, if you remove the "Pope" voice from your head, the voice that tells you: "You must"?

I Choose My Cards In 9 Days

Day 1

Remember when you were a child, you learned through images and stories...

Movie productions are successful because images are worth a thousand words. It is this magic of image that we find in the cards, mixed with a desire to unveil the mysteries inside and outside of us, a desire to connect to what is deeper and sacred.

> What is the impact of imagery on you?

Day 2

Some movies have a greater impact on us, and we remember for a long time – the images, scenes and messages of what we have watched. This is the same for the cards, when we choose decks that resonate with us, their impact is greater.

Your essence and your experiences have an impact on the decks you will choose; some will open your channel of perception, others will enhance your intuition, some will bring you quietness, etc.

> What types of movies do I like?

How can this impact my choices of decks?

Day 3

How to find your deck and how to choose it? We suggest you use your current one to answer these questions that will help you define what your interests are:

- Who are you? And what do you like?
- Example: Do you like architecture or flowers?
- Do you like Star Wars or Indiana Jones?
- Do you like legends or concrete everyday life?

Note:

When I use Mists of Avalon Oracle, I feel Merlin is speaking to me through it ...

When I use the Moonchild Tarot, the Neteru speaks to me through it...

Choosing a Deck that interests you can open your "Channeling abilities" and give spirit words and images they can use to communicate with you.

Day 4

Imagine that you are with a friend, and he tells you about a new brand of shoes that he discovered, chances are that you would buy the same thing at 80% likelihood because you are open to receiving this "subliminal message": It is your friend that you already appreciate who gives you the message + you love shoes!

However, if it is a stranger or an advertiser who tells you about these same shoes, the percentage of you getting the shoe may drop by 20 or 30%: You like shoes but you don't know the guy, and even less of a chance of buying the shoes if you don't like him at all!

Let's transpose this experience to the cards:

If you choose decks that are similar to your friends, this will make you more receptive to their messages!

- Choose 3 friends and identify them with 3 words or more each. Then find a deck that resembles them.

My friend Kiki is gentle, spiritual, angelic, and feminine - she likes white and red and loves painting. She reminds me of the Aura-Soma Tarot!

Day 5

There are millions of possible intentions to work with different decks in your collection. Choose a deck based on how it might match up energetically with your intention. Come back to it in a few weeks or months later to see if you have made progress on it. The danger will be to scatter yourself in several directions, as you work with various intentions and desires at the same time. It's usually best to focus on one intention at a time.

Once you've worked on your intention for a time, check in to see if the particular deck you are using for this goal is collaborating with you in a supportive manner. If there is a feeling of disconnection between the deck and your goal/intention, you might consider changing decks; or it could be that your intention needs to change. In any case, this gives you the choice to decide if you need to release the deck (trade/sell/gift it), or if you can integrate it definitively into your library of decks.

- What is your intention?

To walk in life without intention is to drive a car with a blindfold!

- Clarify your intention by analyzing the cards you got from your draw: Do you want to learn the system? Develop your intuition? Know yourself better? Work with your inner child? Heal the woman and release the rebellious side in yourself? Taming your fears? Understand your emotions? …

Day 6

The vibe of the deck: If you want to be sure the deck speaks to you, watch a YouTube review. You will know it's for you when your heart is quivering, and the images do not leave you.

Try to identify a deck that interests you and find images or a YouTube video about it. Don't buy it directly, but ask about your current cards:

- Why am I interested in this deck?
- What would be the impact on my practice if I get it?
- What would be the impact on my finances?

Day 7

Your deck may take you on another path or take you further than you thought!

When I got the deck of the Victorian Fairies, I wanted to connect with the fairies simply, but the Tarot took me further than I thought: To prepare and offer a course about fairies for 170 people!

Find out what your deck is preparing you to do...

Day 8

Do not compare yourself: We are all part of the human tribe, but we have different Essences and different natures; what you may like will not please another person and it is OK! Be attentive to the facial expressions of clients when you give readings.

Try to accommodate the client's emotions and state of mind when you pick the decks to choose for a reading. You can ask them what deck they would like to use for the session...

> What decks can I use to give readings to accommodate clients?

Day 9

Beware of impulse purchases: You have the right to buy as many cards and decks as you want, if you do it in a conscious, not guilty, and not regrettable way!

Conscious buying is different from impulsive purchase:

> Impulsive purchase:

- You will tend to hide it
- You do it when you feel emotional, fragile, and in pain: it's like going to the grocery store with an empty stomach
- You buy for fear of missing (FOMO syndrome: Fear Of Missing Out)
- You feel guilt and regret after the purchase
- You start to feel the urge to put it away, in order to not remember it

- You feel insecure financially after the purchase
- You look for authorization and many justifications to buy

  - Conscious purchase:
- Allows you to fully appreciate your purchase
- Feeds your soul and allows you to go further
- You feel the pleasure of sharing it with others
- You assume responsibility for the purchase and know what to do with it
- You recognize your RIGHT to buy what pleases you
- You recognize your right to spend your money as you see fit, and you are accountable only to yourself - and to your bills of course!
- You recognize that there are different priorities in your life: finances, food, bills, but also self-care!

  - You identify your emotions and your shadow and work on it...

  - So ... What type of purchase do you usually make?

  - How can you make conscious deck purchases?

Meet with Tarot in 7 Days

Day 1

The Tarot has always been associated with divination but as we saw above the associations that we make with objects depend largely on our practice and our vision of life. Tarot has also been associated with games of chance and more recently with psychological work, for example.

Many theories have been put forward on the origin of the Tarot: Was the Tarot brought by the Saracens? Created by the Chinese? Assembled by Italians or French? Were Minors created first, Majors later? What is the real name: Naib, Tarrochi or Taro?

But what we can see is that the unknown origins of the Tarot add to the mystery which surrounds it and makes us overflow with imagination.

- What is the origin of Tarot? Where does it come from?
- Why was it created?
- What is its place in the divination world?
- What are the different ways to use Tarot? (pick as many cards as you want)
- What can I already do with Tarot?

- What are the "future" possibilities Tarot offers me?
- How can I best use/collaborate with Tarot?

Day 2

Tarot is a marriage between several traditions and cultures; it is not reserved for a country or a nation. It belongs to humanity and continues to cross the physical and temporal barriers to transmit knowledge to us and perhaps hand us the keys to wisdom and knowledge: Knowing who we are and how to navigate this world.

We must therefore not restrict it but allow it to continue its evolution because it will thus meet the needs of present and future times.

- What can help me widen my perception of Tarot?
- How can I help Tarot's evolution?

Day 3

The Tarot is known for its mystical teachings; but in my opinion, it teaches us universality, shows us our change and evolution over time, reminds us of our place in the universe and reconnects us to the sacred even through "ordinary" things of life. Tarot also teaches us to be curious while recognizing our ignorance and accepting it with kindness. As the High Priestess of the Tarot reminds us, everything is not yet revealed to us...

- What does Tarot teach me about:
  - o Humility?
  - o Universality?
  - o The other worlds?

Day 4

Tarot images act on our unconscious: Bring back memories and allow us to express emotions that we can hardly say in words.

- What memories does the Tarot bring back to me now?
- Why?

These memories can come from current life or past lives.

Day 5

In the next chapters, I will share with you some questions and concrete examples of readings. However, I encourage you to interpret the cards on your own, and develop ways using your intuition, based on your symbols, and your memories.

- How can I better trust my abilities to read Tarot?
- How can I build my symbology to read Tarot?
- What can help me strengthen my intuitive abilities?

Day 6

A Tarot deck is made up of 78 cards, each having its own unique meaning. There are 22 Major Arcana cards, 40 Minor Arcana cards and 16 Court cards.

- What is the reason(s) behind this structure?

Day 7

Explore deeper the Tarot System:

- What my intuition is telling me about:
  - Majors?
  - Minors?
  - Court cards?
- What my emotions are telling me about:
  - Majors?
  - Minors?
  - Court cards?
- How can I approach each of them? Pick a card for Majors, one for Minors, and one for Court cards.

Get to Know Your Deck in 21 Days

With this challenge, do not hesitate to use the tracker (you will find it at the end of the book). With this tracker, you will gather all the cards you got, and notice the synchronicities and repetitions.

Week 1: Honeymoon

This is the honeymoon week - we meet the Tarot or Oracle deck for the first time, or we find it after waiting for months and months.

Your deck is your lover

The deck waited so long for your reunion together ... This week, you get to know each other, and as for each love, it is important to know all the strengths and weaknesses of one another...

Day 1

Grab your deck and ask:

- What is the spirit of this deck?
- Does it come with animals, and symbols?
- Is it old? Contemporary? etc.

And if you have more time, here are some bonus questions:

- Its art?
- Does it have extra cards? What do they mean?

Explore the deck and see how:

- It smells...
- Touching it is like ....
- If it was blood, it tastes...
- It reminds me of this movie...
- It reminds me of this music ...

Day 2

- Does your deck carry people?
- How are they: Nice or Scary? Cute or ugly? Sexy or ...

Bonus questions if you have more time:

- What are your main colors?
- What do they mean for **you**?
- What do they mean to **me**?

Day 3

- I'm in love with these cards: What cards do you most like in this deck? Why?
- These cards freak me out: What cards do you like the least or make you uncomfortable? Why?

Bonus questions if you have many decks:

- #TarotCombo: What other Oracle or Tarot decks can you combine with this deck?

Day 4

- When is the best time to meet with this deck? Pick a card or more. Is it day or night? Every day or every 2 days? Or more?

Day 5

What is the expertise of this deck: Relationships? Work? Shadow work? Or just gossiping and chatting!

Pick a card or more.

Day 6

Ok, now lets' get serious:

- Why did this deck enter your life: Why is it here at this specific moment?
- What do you need to know from this deck?
- What work will you do together?
- And by the way... what does he think about you? Yes, decks have opinions, too!

Day 7

- What did you learn about this deck during this first week?
- What did you learn about yourself this week?
- What is your conclusion about your Honeymoon week?

Bonus questions if you have a Tarot deck:

- What are the main suits?
- How is the Royal Family?

Week 2: Let's Live Together

This week, you will go further with your deck. Beyond the romantic beginnings, you will need to experience serious things together, just like couples: You will talk about money and cleaning the dishes, about children and work... So, this week you will learn more about the deck: You will be together night and day, and through that, you learn more about it...

Day 1

Before you go to sleep: Tell your deck: "I would love to have you in my bed tonight! So, let's spend the night together."

Put your deck under your pillow or by your side and let it guide you through your dreams...

When you wake up, record your dream, sensations, images, and anything that triggered you!

Day 2

Ask your deck these questions:

- How are we doing together this week?
- What does your deck need? A crystal? To be charged in the Moon?
- Or ... well, another night with you?

Day 3

Let's make a non-sense story together:

- If you are doing this challenge alone: Pick one card at a time and tell your story - it doesn't need to make sense - the goal is to have FUN!
- If you are doing this challenge in the Facebook group, follow the story that is being displayed. Pick a card and add your part to that story.

Day 4

When we live as a couple for a long time, we may lose passion and we can start looking for a new adventure! Or we may look for new activities to do